DREAM EXPRESS

Len Jenkin

BROADWAY PLAY PUBLISHING INC
New York
www.broadwayplaypublishing.com
info@broadwayplaypublishing.com

First printing: February 2014
I S B N: 978-0-88145-553-3

Book design: Marie Donovan
Page make-up: Adobe Indesign
Typeface: Palatino
Printed and bound in the U S A

ABOUT THE AUTHOR

Len Jenkin's plays include DARK RIDE, TIME IN
KAFKA, AMERICAN NOTES, PILGRIMS OF THE
NIGHT, CARELESS LOVE, MY UNCLE SAM, LIMBO
TALES, PSALM 151, and LIKE I SAY. His works for
the stage, often directed by him, have been produced
throughout the United States, as well as in England,
France, Denmark, Germany and Japan. His adaptations
for the stage include Voltaire's CANDIDE (Guthrie
Theater, Minneapolis), Aristophanes' THE BIRDS
(Yale Repertory Theater, New Haven), and Kafka's A
COUNTRY DOCTOR (Classic Stage Company, New
York).

His novel N Judah is currently available in bookstores
and on the web at lenjenkin.com. He has also worked
in television and for feature films.

He has received three OBIE awards for Directing and
Playwriting, a Guggenheim Fellowship, a Rockefeller
Foundation Award, a nomination for an Emmy
Award, the Helen Merrill Award, and four National
Endowment for the Arts Fellowships.

He teaches in the Dramatic Writing Department, Tisch
School of the Arts, New York University.

The original and ongoing group that creates THE DREAM EXPRESS consists of Len Jenkin, John Kilgore, Steve Mellor, and Deirdre O'Connell.

SPIN MILTON.. Steve Mellor
MARLENE MILTON...............................Deirdre O'Connell

Writing & direction...Len Jenkin
Music composition & sound design .... John Kilgore
Set .... Len Jenkin, Steve Mellor
Costumes........................Deirdre O'Connell, Steve Mellor

CHARACTERS & SETTING

Marlene Milton
Spin Milton

Spin and Marlene Miltcn *are a performing duo,* Spin
on keyboard and vocals, Marlene *on vocals and occasional
keyboard. They're no longer young, still hip, down but by no
means out.*

Uncle Wolfie is a voice on the phone. He can be pre-recorded.

Time: Now. Night.

Place: A stage or bandstand, somewhere in America.

A NOTE ON MUSIC

Every night in America, a thousand cover bands play recent pop tunes and oldies in clubs and pay nothing. This is probably illegal, but no one's watching, and at that level, no one cares. There's no money in it.

The Dream Express suggests that if you're making decent money doing our show, you get permission from the original artists or their representatives to use their work. If that permission is too expensive, don't use that song.

Our own original music you have already gotten permission to use by getting permission to do the show.

In the lists before the "Additional Songs and Stories" section, all the music is labeled as cover, original, traditionals, or dream version (new lyrics).

For use of our music for DREAM EXPRESS, original songs and cover versions, contact John Kilgore at JohnKilgore@earthlink.net.

A NOTE ON TEXT

This book has two parts: "SET 1" and "Additional Songs and Stories". This is all the materials created for DREAM EXPRESS as the show developed and changed. SET 1 is the original version. Each time we performed the show we would create new material, insert it and drop some of the old songs and/or stories. This text intends to offer the opportunity to anyone intending to do the show to create the version they want to do. Shuffle the cards, any way that works for you and your creative team.

A NOTE ON AUTHORSHIP

Steve Mellor wrote the lyrics for *Fuck You, I'm A Millionaire, Dead Boys Don't Cry* and *I Get Drunk On Christmas.* He also wrote the text for "Roger Harvey's Brain" and "Woman And The Devil By The Railroad Tracks". Deirdre O'Connell wrote the lyrics for *Marlene And The Devil.*

All remaining text and original lyrics are by Len Jenkin. However, all four partners in DREAM EXPRESS had enormous input into everything we did, and work would often change in rehearsal. The extent to which DREAM EXPRESS was (and is) a group effort can't be overstated.

For Deirdre O'Connell, Steve Mellor, and John Kilgore

This work is for my collaborators, over 15 years. Like fine wine, we keep getting better with age.

And in memory of John Nesci, our Uncle Wolfie.

SET 1

(Train sound)

*(*MARLENE MILTON *and* SPIN MILTON *appear on stage.)*

*(*SPIN *sits at an electronic keyboard and rhythm machine.* MARLENE *stands alongside him. Both of them have mikes.)*

(It's late at night, somewhere in America.)

SPIN: Good evening. On behalf of the Uncle Remus Motel, I'd like to welcome you all to the Briarpatch Lounge. I'm Spin Milton, and this is my lovely ex-wife Marlene. But that's just a label. The label on the bottle, not the juice inside. And as most of you out there already know, we're THE DREAM EXPRESS.
Tonite means a lot to me. It's kind of our anniversary. We've been at the Briarpatch for exactly three months now. Three pretty terrific months. Isn't that right, Marlene?

MARLENE: Some kind of wonderful...

SPIN: You know, only a few of you out there know this, but I was raised in a state orphanage and after that, an endless series of foster homes. For me, the late night crowd that pulls in here off Central for a little warmth, a little musical sharing—is the only real family I've ever known.
A little musical sharing... You know, sharing is caring. Total sharing is total caring. Hey, the truth is you can say it all in three little words. God—Love—Acid.

Hey, just kidding. Those days are gone, right—but not forgotten.

Thank you all, a very real thank you, for being with Marlene, and me, and our music.

This is Spin Milton reminding you again, in case your mind is a little fried, a little shaky tonite-a nite where the outlines blur, things slide into one another—that hand resting on the thin rayon fabric of her skirt, touching the warm thigh beneath, that hand just dissolves into her flesh, flesh to flesh. A meltdown.

MARLENE: Relax. Don't let Spin make you nervous. It doesn't matter. We're all one body anyway. THE body. And while you come to terms with that one, I'll remind you that we are the DREAM EXPRESS. We hope you're having as much fun as we are.

SPIN: You paid for the whole seat, but you'll only use the edge, edge, edge…

MARLENE: You know, I've heard many people speak words of love. I've seen them wash the car with a green garden hose in a green shade and short shorts in the sunset. In the scented nighttime, they rub up against each other, make true love, and watch a Godzilla movie on the late show. It's bend over Red Rover, and in the shimmery glimmer of the morning after, whenever it may fall—somebody look over their shoulder and somebody gone, with a heigh-di-ho and a fare-thee-well.

Hey, my friends—who knows what is in anybody's heart?

SPIN: It's a mystery.

MARLENE: Bees make honey, even in the lion's ear.

SPIN: You know, whoever you are, the very fact that you're sitting here tonight implies that you may very well have ruined your whole fucking life already. Don't you just know it. I know it. I know the shit

you *think.* Don't smile, sweetheart. You're not on
the outside, looking in the cage. These remarks are
inclusive. Good looks don't get you off this time.

MARLENE: That's right.

SPIN: I *know* what's in that nighttable drawer, and in
the trunk of the Chevrolet Caprice. I know what it
takes sometimes to get you through till dawn.
I love you. Anyway. So does Marlene. That little candle
is still burning, you know, the one you lit in a dream
when you were five years old. That's why we're here.
A little tenderness. Open your heart, and let us in.
Ready, Marlene.

MARLENE: Ready, baby.

SPIN: Let's do it like we did it in Memphis. When that
train came, we were already gone…

(Music)

(Dream Express sings and plays)

Let's Get Physical (Milton Version)

SPIN: You're liking all the things that you know I'll say
Cause I make stimulating conversation
I gotta handle you just right
I know what you mean

You took me to a Polynesian restaurant
(Tell me Samoa)
Then to a Lithuanian movie
(Viva Vilnius, baby)
There's nothing left to talk about except horizontally

Let's get physical, physical
I wanna get physical
Let's get into physical
Let me hear your body talk, your body talk
Let me hear your body talk

Now Miss Universe, let me talk to your mind for a
minute
I been patient, I been good
Two total strangers on a table
I been a doorknob in a golden room
I know what you mean
You think I'll understand your point of view
(That's right, baby,)
'Cause we know each other mentally
Can you conceive that you're bringin' out
The animal in me

Let's get animal, animal
I wanna get animal
Let's get into animal
Let me hear your body talk, your body talk...

And so we watched in amazement
As the miller told his tale
As her face at first just ghostly
Turned a whiter shade of pale
Doot doot doot doo doo doot etc....

(End music)

MARLENE: Thank you, thank you so much. We're so
glad to be back at the Shalimar Lounge. Our music
communicates best when we work downtown—
between the check cashing place and the Blood Donor
Center. Between the Jack in the Box and the Interstate
Off-Ramp. You know, this town is clinging to the
planet by its teeth. Everybody let go and float up to
heaven—or tumble ass backwards into the abyss.
The fact is, it's a tad slow out there on the main stem.
We seem to be here, but where the hell is everyone
else?
I remember now. They're all gathered around the town
well...

(Music)

(Dream Express sings and plays.)

Town Well

SPIN: Hey Sugar, you wanna go for a drive? We wheel 'round to my place, I got the V C R repaired so we can view a fuck movie. They got em down the store twenty four so whatddaya whatddaya whatddaya say? It ain't love but it ain't bad.

MARLENE: What? *(Laughs)*

SPIN: You can't stand there with your girlfriends forever, man. Those bitches are stupid.

(Music continuing under. SPIN sobs into the mike, a child crying.)

MARLENE: Mommy's only gonna be inna Price-Chopper for a minit. You jus' wait inna car, O K? You'll be all right. And stay outta the damn glovebox. Mommy's got her private stuff in there.

SPIN: *(As a child in tears)* I wanna go inna Pirce-Chopper with Mommy...

MARLENE: Ahma bring you sompin. Bag o those toasted chitos. What kind you want? They got em cool ranch style? Old fashioned cheese? Chimichanga?

SPIN: *(As child, crying louder than before)* I wanna go inna Price-Chopper with mommmy!

MARLENE: Shit.

(Music continuing under...)

SPIN: I'm an old man, an old old man and I'm blind. Lost my sight in a work related accident. Jones and Laughlin never gave me a dime. Fuck it's my negligence. Have a drink in the parking lot don't mean I can't run the damn roller.
I worked hard in my day. Worked like a fucking cart horse and broke my health. Now I ain't even got a

decent place to flop. I gotta go hunting me a rat hole at night.

MARLENE: Hey, I'm sorry. I really am. I...

SPIN: A man can't get a square deal in this world. There ain't no justice in this world.

MARLENE: She is a hard life, my friend.

SPIN: No justice and no mercy.
I'd drag my balls across broken glass just to finger-fuck your shadow...

(Music continuing under...)

MARLENE: Hey, babe, how you doin'? *(No answer)* I *said,* how you doin'?

SPIN: Doin' my wash.

MARLENE: Believe it or not, I *knew* that. I haven't seen you around before.

SPIN: I just hit the rinse cycle here...

MARLENE: Hey, I apologize. Please. I mis-spoke. Forgive me. What I meant to ask was, who the fuck are you?

SPIN: Hey, take it easy, lady. No law says I gotta talk to everybody.

MARLENE: This is not a legal question. It's about you being a rude asshole.
(Sweetly) So?

SPIN: I'm just a guy, just a guy around here.

MARLENE: That's interesting conversation, all right. So, uh, what do you do?

SPIN: What do you mean, what do I *do*?

MARLENE: Hearing problem is it? What do you do?

SPIN: I hang around the Launderama, watch college girls fold their underwear with my dick hid inna box of Tide.

MARLENE: Talk dirty to decent people, someone's gonna put your head through the wall. You g_et_ that?

SPIN: Hey, I was kidding, lady. A joke. I'm a student, O K. Down the T I A.

MARLENE: T I A?

SPIN: Technical Institute of America. That's the college, down on Central. I start next week, if my loan comes through. I'm gonna study computers. What makes the screen light up. How they actually work, you know.

MARLENE: Well, Mister College Student, here's my idea. We leave the wash to spin the fuck around and we drop in the liquor store buy a quart of Sweet Leilani, you come over, we drink it up, lay you down on my sofa, close your eyes and have the nicest li'l dream…

(End music)

SPIN: Once again, we're all here. In the Tiger's Eye. On the wobbling pivot.

MARLENE: And while you get your balancing act together…

SPIN: Equilibrate yourselves.

MARLENE: …let me remind you that we're the Dream Express. I'm Marlene Milton, and the gentleman on my right is…

SPIN: Spin Milton, alias Long John the Doctor. I'm not the doctor for what you think is wrong with you—I'm the doctor for what *is* wrong with you. *(Looks crowd over)* Hmmmm. Open wide. Say AHHH. Ah ha. You got love trouble.

Just take a red onion, half a glass of turpentine, and a pinch of Uncrossing Powder Number Nine. Grind it up in the cuisinart with some fine Colombian coffee beans and a spoonful of your pubic hair. Brew by the drip method, sweeten liberally and serve hot when the lady or gentleman comes to call.

MARLENE: Get some, and get it *right* this time. Help is at hand. Lucky dogs, all of you.

SPIN: Lucky lucky dogs.

MARLENE: Long John the Doctor is *in*.

SPIN: All my prescriptions can be filled by the pharmaceutical division of the Seven Spanish Powers Curio Shop.

MARLENE: La Botanica Latina.

SPIN: Near the railroad tracks outside of Corpus Christi, Texas. If they don't have it, they'll go out and get it, and if it can't be got, they'll make it up in the bathtub.

MARLENE: Es muy muy muy barato.

SPIN: Now let's just say I fix you. The one you desire becomes your love slave.

MARLENE: Esclavo amoroso.

SPIN: They're lying in bed right next to you, naked and exhausted, snoring into the pillow. But you're wide awake. Clock says three a.m. And you're covered in sweat. Your body's shaking and your brain is on fire. 'Nother little nightmare. Pain and Death tearing at you with their yellow fingernails—and your wrinkled old Mom and Dad, your beautiful children, even your new lover, they're all around you, hopping on one leg and gnashing their teeth. They suffer, moaning with grief and madness. In the background, a great mob of people you don't even know are drowning in a senseless lake of sorrow. The green ball is spinning out of control.

Why've you been dropped off here? Some kind of failed experiment? Who *are* you, anyway? Not a clue. What's gonna happen to you tomorrow, or in thirty years, and is it gonna *hurt*?

MARLENE & SPIN: Nobody cares.

(MARLENE *blows a kiss to the audience.*)

SPIN: What you really got, the sickness that's creeping in your window at night, that lives in your underwear, that's walking behind you so you're scared to look back over your shoulder—that's Amnesia. You forget who you are. If you're a bad case, so does everyone else. Get any worse, *I'm* gonna forget who you are. So is Nurse Marlene.

MARLENE: Who are you?

SPIN: Amnesia is not a disease—it's a condition. You don't need to catch it—you got it. Amnesia is your birthright in the U S A. And if you don't remember you got it, you got the worst case of all.

(*Siren sound*)

SPIN: There's an ambulance. You need not ask for whom the red light flashes…

MARLENE: You, baby.
Call for the doctor.

SPIN: Call for the nurse.

MARLENE: Call for the lady with the alligator purse.

SPIN: I'm Spin Milton, A K A Long John your barefoot medical practitioner, and for each and every case of amnesia—I got the cure.

(MARLENE *and* SPIN *look over the crowd.*)

SPIN: See me between sets, darling.

MARLENE: You interested, Chief? See the Doctor after the show.

SPIN: See me later, sweetheart. Backstage.

(Music under...)

MARLENE: For everyone in trouble, a love song. *Un chanson d'amour.*

SPIN: *Il pleure dans mon coeur commme il pleut sur la ville, bebe.*

(Music)

MUSIC EXPRESS: *(Sings and plays)*

The Pina Colada Song (Milton Version)

SPIN: I was tired of my lady
The bitch had made me insane
I was lost.
My life was a lie.
Lying next to her made my flesh crawl
So while she lay there sleeping
I read the paper in bed
And in the personal column
Was this letter I read

MARLENE & SPIN:

If you like pina coladas
Getting lost on a train
If you're not into health food
If you have half a brain

MARLENE: If you like making love at midnite

SPIN: Ah ha...

MARLENE: In the dunes on the Cape

SPIN: P-town!

MARLENE: I'm the one that you've looked for

SPIN: That's in Massachusetts.

MARLENE: Bring electrical tape.

SPIN: Wow!

MARLENE: He didn't think about his lady

SPIN: Rhonda, the bitch!

MARLENE: I know that sounds kinda mean

SPIN: This ad was meant for me alone.

MARLENE: For him and his old lady

SPIN: Someone is strangling swans…

MARLENE: Had fallen into the same old dull routine

SPIN: In the Bois de Boulogne

MARLENE: So he wrote to the paper

SPIN: That's in Gay Paree

MARLENE: Took out a personal ad
And though he's nobody's poet

SPIN: Log, dog.

MARLENE: He thought it wasn't half bad

MARLENE & SPIN: Yes I like pina coladas
And I have half a brain
I'm not much into tofu
And the dog's a Great Dane

SPIN: I've got to meet you by tomorrow noon
Or else I'm gonna go ape
At an eatery called Denny's
I'll bring electrical tape

MARLENE: So he waited with high hopes

SPIN: I brought my pistol too

MARLENE: And she walked in the place

SPIN: Fourteen shot clip

MARLENE: He knew her smile in an instant

SPIN: Hi! My name's…

MARLENE: He knew the curve of my face

SPIN: Oh my God…

MARLENE: I was his own lovely lady

SPIN: Rhonda!

(End music)

MARLENE: And I said— Oh, it's you, Nelson. You put an ad in the paper, you dweebhead. Were you gonna fuck her, Nelson?

SPIN: I brought my pistol, Rhonda.

MARLENE: Oh. Are you gonna kill me, Nelson? Are you gonna kill me, Nelson? Are you gonna kill me, Nelson? Bring it on, baby. Bring it on!

(Shootout at Dennys: gunfire, screams:)

CROWD: *(On tape)* Oh my God! He's got a gun! Do fries go wid dat shake? Get the children under the table! Charlene, can we get a mop out here? Oh god oh god oh god. Is that ketchup or what? What!

MARLENE: Missed me, Nelson.

ANNOUNCER: *(On tape)* Singing Duo Survives Shootout! Film at eleven!

MARLENE: I don't like pina coladas. I like sad carnivals, drawings of the devil, extravagant operas, childhood storybooks, religious wars, living rooms at the bottom of lakes, fog, black silk sheets, churches, snow.

(End song)

SPIN: Thank you.

MARLENE: Thank you very much. We are the Dream Express.

SPIN: And we're coming around a curve here at the Jack O' Hearts Lounge, the fully mentholated nitespot of the Royal Flush Travel-lodge.

MARLENE: You know, only a few of you out there know this, but last summer Spin and me were heading west on I-Forty in this old Plymouth Duster. It's three a.m. And I'm half asleep, and right where the road curves down under viaduct, we get hit broadside by a ten-ton semi hauling strawberries in from Mexico.
I lay there in the front seat, covered with glass and blood. Spin was trapped behind the twisted steering wheel, and he's moaning. The truck driver gets out of the cab, steps into the headlights. He's got a girl with him, maybe eighteen. They look at us bleed. "Madre de Dios" he says to her. "Let's get the fuck out of here." Then I heard a siren, and I passed out.

(Music begins under.)

MARLENE: Intensive Care Unit. Sunrise, some intern with a babyface and pale blue eyes looked down at me. "Wheel away the paddles," he said. "The chick's a goner. No need to defibrillate dead meat."
Then I floated up to the ceiling and looked down on Spin and me. Spin had six tubes coming outta him. He was pale, like he'd been drained of blood, and I could see the breath shake his chest as he gasped for air. Suddenly there was a high pitched sucking sound like an industrial vacuum cleaner, and I was outta there, my bed soaring out the window like a child's dream. Next thing you know, I'm in a golden room. My Grandma Gussie comes in from the kitchen. She hands me a cold colacoko in a jelly glass. Then she smiles a beautiful smile in her wrinkly face.

SPIN: *(Echoing under, soft)* Marlene…Marlene…

MARLENE: You ever wonder what the dead might have to say? A lot. "Shut up, Grandma," I finally said, "and just tell me—what secrets do the dead know that the living don't?" She tried to answer me, but her head burst into flames. Grandma's voice called to me out of her burning head. She was trying to reach me, to tell me...

SPIN: *(Echoing under, more and more insistent)* Marlene... Marlene...MARLEEEEEENE.

MARLENE: SPIIIIIIIIN!

(Music ends.)

MARLENE: I wanted to stay with Spin. We're not finished here yet.
I came to, with all functions reading normal. I'd been dead for seven minutes.
The doctors didn't know how I made it back. Jerks. Irreversible brain damage, my ass.

(MARLENE exits. SPIN doodles at the keyboard.)

(Music—SPIN's riff)

SPIN: Here's a little riff I learned from a gentleman by the name of Mister Groove Holmes, king of the funky-butt organ. *(He doodles some more.)*

(End music.)

SPIN: Same train, different time... A young girl is standing by the side of a low-country road in the evening. Its misty, little chill in the air, and she's just standing there in the sawgrass with a sleeveless dress on. A white party dress, like she's going somewhere. I pull over. "Where you headed?" I say. She says "Nowhere in particular." I say "I'm going down to this dance by the water. You wanna go?" She gets in and folds her hands in her lap. We barely spoke all the way to the beach. They had this dancefloor near the ocean, colored lights strung up everywhere. Christmas in the summertime. Rock and roll music, some local radio station playing.
There's a fried clam shack on a pier out over the water. We walk out to the far end of the pier. No one else around, and the surf's running dark underneath us. A

boat goes by with a green light on the stern, way out on the black water.

I kissed her. After a long moment, she pulls away. They play a slow one, and we dance.

MARLENE: *(Sings)* "The ship of love, carried you from me, ooh ooh oooh ooh
But I'll always love you, for eternity
I spend my nights, by the lonely sea
Wondering are you thinking, are you thinking of me…"

SPIN: On the way home, she asks to ride in the back seat. She's quiet. I keep checking the rear view mirror to see if she's really there. Then we hit an empty stretch of road, no lights, no other cars, and she starts to sing.

MARLENE: *(Singing very softly)*
"I spend my nites by the lonely sea Wondering are you thinking, are you thinking of me…"

SPIN: And then I'm not driving anymore. I'm going down the same road, but I'm on horseback. I'm riding bareback, one hand twisted up in the horse's mane with her behind me, body pressed to mine, arms tight around my waist. The horse gallops down the road like a mad thing.

Her warm breath is in my ear. She whispers…

MARLENE: *(Whisper)* I won't ever forget you, Spin. Not ever, ever, ever.

SPIN: And she laughs. That laugh will be a bell ringing in the clouds when my children and myself are dust. She gets out, and I hear the car door slam shut behind me. She walks away through the mist and the sawgrass into darkness.

I sit there till the sun comes up, waiting for nothing.

(Music)

(Dream Express sings and plays)

Wear Your Love Like Heaven (Milton Version)

Color sky prussian blue
Scarlet cheese changes you
Crimson ball sinks from view
Wear your love like heaven
Wear your love like heaven
Wear your love like heaven

(Phone rings under)

Lord kiss me once more, fill me with song, Allah
Kiss me once more, that I may, that I may
Wear my love like heaven
Wear my love like heaven
Wear my love like heaven
La la la la la la la la la

*(MARLENE and SPIN each sing a difference verse,
simultaneously. One of them's singing the wrong one. A
phone still rings somewhere.)*

SPIN: Color sky Havana lake
Color sky rose carmethine
Alizarine crimson

(As MARLENE sings)

MARLENE: Canna believe what I see
All I have wished for will be
All our race proud and free
Wear your love like heaven
Wear your love like heaven
Wear your love like heaven

*(Phone rings louder, drowning out music and song.
MARLENE and SPIN stop singing and playing. End music.
Phone continues ringing, then a click of connection.)*

WOLFIE: *(On phone)* Gotcha! At last. Bust my balls over
the luminous…
Spin? You with me?

SPIN: Yeah, Wolfie.

WOLFIE: Bust my balls over the luminous phonelines surfing the infinite web to find you.

SPIN: Uncle Wolfie, our manager.

WOLFIE: I'm as good as ever, but somehow, somehow my coffee's getting weak here. It's your goddamn fault. The two of you are fucking hopeless.
Marlene, you there?

MARLENE: I'm here, Wolfie.

WOLFIE: *(Sings)* "I'm the pied piper, follow me, I'm the pied piper, trust in me, and I'll show you, where its at, hey come on babe, follow me, I'm the pied piper, trust in me..."
Let's hallucinate together, shall we? About Des Moines Iowa. The River West Club.

SPIN: Oh man, I took a bullet there...

WOLFIE: Two weeks from now. See...uh...

MARLENE: Manny.

WOLFIE: ...Manny.

MARLENE: Wolfie, you're fucking with us. Manny doesn't pay up. He hasn't paid us yet for the gig last March, and...

WOLFIE: Doubt insults me. Like Jesus said to Thomas, a doubting woman is not gonna swing with the angel band. If you be the Jesus take the thorns from off your head? Is that what it was about, getting the damn thorns off? Making miracles, while Papa Joe still pulls a sixteen hour shift down at the pretzel factory. Twist! Twist! Twist! Like we did last summer, and the summer before, a hundred and ten in the fucking shade. Is it about where's my railroad ticket and my blue serge suit? Or is it about transforming this endless suffering into some kind of fucking grace?
Marlene, You still there?

MARLENE: Yeah, Wolfie. I'm still here.

WOLFIE: Remember the motto of every great artiste—
"Make 'em laugh, make 'em cry, make 'em kiss ten
bucks goodbye."
Send a check to your Uncle Wolfie.

(Phone goes dead. buzzing sound. Click)

(Music)

(Dream Express sings and plays)

Fuck You, I'm a Millionaire

I know that it's me that you can't stand
But I got money in a suitcase, twice five hundred grand
So if you don't like me, I don't care
Fuck you, I'm a millionaire

I got bank accounts in Switzerland, hotels in
Martinique
I have five Eurasian girlfriends who come in twice a
week
You say that you don't like me, ask me if I care
Fuck you, I'm a millionaire

There's a couple dozen senators, with whom I often
dine
There's nine supreme court justices and all of them are
mine
My memos to the president have a literary flair
They say, Fuck me, I'm a millionaire

The hobo on the corner says
"Got a nickel you can spare?"
I say Fuck you, I'm a millionaire. Fuck you. Fuck you.
Fuck you! Fuck you!
Hey where you from? Ohio?
Why don't you get fucked.
Tax breaks for me
Family values for you!
Fuck you. Fuck you!

(End music)

SPIN: I got an inspiration I wanna share with all of you, and I'm sure you're gonna enjoy it. Why don't you clean yourself up, buy yourself some flowers, take yourself out to a show or a movie, buy yourself a couple of drinks afterwards, take yourself home, crawl into bed, and

MARLENE & SPIN: FUCK YOURSELF.

(End song)

MARLENE: Thank you.

SPIN: We're gonna take a little break, that little pause that refreshes. We are the DREAM EXPRESS, the rockin railroad, the midnite liner, keeping all our friends out there, keeping all of you, and you know who you are, keeping you *on track*. We'll be right back, so don't go home. Nothing there but your empty bed. You go home, we'll come find you. You wake up, it's four a.m. And there's Marlene, sitting on the end of your bed sucking on a Salem lite 100, and I'm in the corner by that beat up dresser, stark naked, and I'm *plugging in.*

MARLENE: While the Dream Express is out in the alley, getting itself back on track, maybe all of you can spend a little time together.

SPIN: Love will find a way. We'll be right back...

(MARLENE and SPIN go off, and immediately reappear—a very quick "intermission", about 10 seconds.)

MARLENE: We're back. Back from the deeps of space, back from the very lip of the void—and you're still here.

SPIN: Worn out your welcome in the rest of the universe?

MARLENE: Doesn't matter. Here at Pepper's Town and Country, we take your presence as a profound compliment to the band, and we respect the precious gift of your—attention.

SPIN: We're conveniently located in the Asteroid Belt, the place of broken shells. A world that didn't quite measure up, but out of pity God couldn't throw it away.
We're here for you, baby. Sharing is caring, and total sharing is total caring.

MARLENE: You're riding in a club car on the Dream Express, and we're way over the speed limit. You can't call home anymore, Charlie. Spin has cut the lines.

(Music begins.)

(Dream Express talks overa nd with the music)

Charlie

MARLENE: Woman at the next table leans toward you. Smell the perfume. Somethin' you remember? Ambush? Tabu? Rotting meat? She got one of those faces they pay people for and she says, "Let's go someplace nice."

SPIN: Go on, Charlie. We'll take care of the bill. Follow her.

MARLENE: Slip out that side door, Charlie. Look for your car in the parking lot. Uh oh. Your car's not there, Charlie. Matter of fact, the parking lot's not there. That girl's not there anymore.

SPIN: What the fuck...?

MARLENE: You're on the street, Charlie, downtown, in some kinda city. There's a dump called the Elk Hotel next to a sort of Moorish arcade made out of popsicle sticks with a green light coming out of it, as if the interior of the arcade was beneath the sea. On

the far side is a lingerie shop—Celeste's Nights of
Desire Boutique. The boutique is still closed, but the
key, the key is in your hand. You're wearing a flower
print dress, and red pumps. You've got a lifestyle here,
Charlie. I mean, Celeste.

SPIN: Go inside, girlfriend.

(MARLENE *steps forward.*)

MARLENE: Smells like rotting meat in here.

(*The phone rings.*)

(MARLENE *picks up the phone.*)

SPIN: (*On phone*) Celeste? Don't forget that potluck
party tonight. And don't wear those red pumps. You
look like a whore. Oh, and the kitchen sink's backed up
again. Some kind of animal is living in the pipes. And
some doctor called, says he needs to talk to you about
biopsy results. Oh and everyone you know is dead,
and the world is on fire. *Celeste? Celeste?*

(*Music ends.*)

SPIN: There's been a mistake here. Hasn't there? I
mean, in regard to your life. Things not turning out the
way they should. Don't get bitter about it. No one ever
knows what's actually shaking. And that's quite all
right. It's O K.

MARLENE: A-O K.

SPIN: It's O K.
Picture this.

MARLENE: In your mind, Charlie.

SPIN: Spin and Marlene Milton are in the back seat,
and Uncle Wolfie's at the wheel. They're coming outta
Fort Worth, on their way to Amarillo for a week at the
Hi-Hat Lounge. Been driving all night, and about ten
o'clock in the morning Uncle Wolfie pulls around to
the rear entrance of the Hi-Hat.

MARLENE: *(As Wolfie)* Sound check. Come on, darlings.

SPIN: No answer.

Wolfie gets out, opens a rear door of the Buick.
Marlene's body rolls out into the gutter.

MARLENE: *(As Wolfie)* Stoned again.

SPIN: Wolfie leans into the back seat. Spin's lying there
with his mouth open. A fly lands on his tongue.

MARLENE: *(As Wolfie)* Oh, shit.

SPIN: Their dealer gave them a bad bag. Double
overdose. Spin and Marlene Milton, the Dream
Express, died in the back seat of a Buick on the way to
a club date in Texas.
Uncle Wolfie's first thought was

MARLENE: *(As Wolfie)* Five nights five hundred a night
out the fucking window. Money in the grave.

SPIN: Uncle Wolfie was broke. He looked at the
corpses.

MARLENE: *(As Wolfie)* Stupid junkies.

SPIN: Then he got an idea.

MARLENE: *(As Wolfie)* Ah hah!

SPIN: He got behind the wheel, drove out to a picnic
spot he knew by the banks of the Ohio. He stripped the
bodies, tied on enough concrete to keep them down
in the mud with the catfish, and rolled them into the
river. Spin and Marlene. There they go—

MARLENE: Bye, bye.

MARLENE & SPIN: See them suffer a sea change, into
something rich and strange. Sea nymphs hourly ring
their knell.

SPIN: Hark, I hear them.

MARLENE: Ding, dong, bell.

SPIN: Uncle Wolfie made it to a pay phone. Two calls. I was at the Hi-Hat in twenty minutes. She was already in the dressing room, combing out her auburn hair.

MARLENE: *(Her younger self)* Hi.

SPIN: *(His younger self)* Hi.

MARLENE: You got a cigarette?

SPIN: Uncle Wolfie came in.

MARLENE: *(As Wolfie)* Here's the deal, you two. SINGING DUO SURVIVES CAR WRECK! A MIRACLE! Newspapers'll be here in a minute. You two are now the...

MARLENE & SPIN: Dream Express.

MARLENE: So you see, we are shadows. See right through us. Shadows of a duo who, for all we know, were also shadows. Someday we'll make a wrong turn, and our manager will make two more phone calls. Who knows for how many centuries Uncle Wolfie has been riding on the Dream Express.
Here's a love song.

(Music)

DREAM EXPRESS: *(Sings and plays)*

Changes (Milton Version)

SPIN: Everyone is going through changes
And no one knows what's going on
Everybody changes places
But the world still carries on

MARLENE & SPIN: Love must always turn to sorrow
And everyone must play the game
It's here today and gone tomorrow
But the world goes on the same

MARLENE: Love must always turn to sorrow
And everyone must play the game

It's here today and gone tomorrow
But the world goes on the same

(End music.)

SPIN: *(Whisper)* Thank you.

(End music. SPIN *exits.)*

MARLENE: First time I saw Spin he was standing on
the streetcorner in the falling snow, with a little casio
keyboard hooked up to a speaker, and he's standing
there in a thin coat with his toes peeking outta his
hightops and a scraggly beard, and I see him reach
over on the street for a butt and he lites it up. He's
maybe twenty. I'm seventeen at the time, and I'm
working. This is my lunch hour. I'm working at the
Taco Bell. Chimichanga? Chimichanga? I'm not like the
other kids on the line. I'm full time so I can get enough
money to buy a car, drive outta town so fast they'll
think I dematerialized. Say, Janet, where's Marlene?
See those two red lights in the dark. Look at 'em get
smaller. That's Marlene's spirit body out on I-40.
Smaller and smaller. Now she's gone. Bye bye.
So there he is, this very beautiful boy standing in the
snow like a jerk, and now he's singing this dumb
sixties song.

(Music. SPIN *returns, sings.)*

(Dream Express sings and plays)

Walk Away Renee (Milton Version)

SPIN: And when I see the sign that points one way

MARLENE: I know that one…

SPIN: The one we used to pass by every day

MARLENE: So I join in

MARLENE & SPIN: Just walk away, Renee
You won't see me follow you back home
The empty sidewalks on my block are not the same

You're not to blame…
From deep inside the tears I'm forced to cry
From deep inside the pain I chose to hide
Just walk away, Renee
You won't see me follow you back home
Now that the rain beats down, upon my weary eyes
For me it cries.

(Music continuing under…)

MARLENE: We start talking, and we're talking about stuff, like movies, an' he says

SPIN: You got any cigarettes?

MARLENE: Yeah, but I'm sorry they're menthol. Kools. *(Shows pack)*

SPIN: That's my brand. *(Shows crumpled up empty pack)*

(Both take a cigarette from MARLENE's pack.)

MARLENE: We light up.

(MARLENE and SPIN light up.)

MARLENE: Cigarette party.
We don't have anything else to say.
Nobody's passing by to give any money for music cause the weather's so lousy.
But we just stay there sucking in the smoke, and the snow's falling all around. I'm freezing, and I think he is too but he won't say anything…

(End music)

MARLENE: I got a place. It's warm there. You wanna come over?

SPIN: She takes my arm and we walk. After awhile we come to this old red brick building between two factories and we walk up to the fourth floor. We go into her apartment. It's a hole in the wall, but she's got it fixed up clean and pretty. She's got a single bed, with

some kind of guatemalan rug or something over it, and
a beat up stuffed squirrel on top.

MARLENE: Living room, bedroom, kitchen.
Simultaneously. You like it?

SPIN: Yeah. I like it.

MARLENE: Really? You really like it.

SPIN: Looks like a mansion to me.

MARLENE: I'm a little behind in the rent. The landlady's
been getting on me lately.

SPIN: It's hard times for a lot of people. I'd like to give
you some money, but I don't have…

MARLENE: Hey, I'm just talking about how things are,
O K? I didn't invite you here to ask you for anything.

SPIN: I didn't think that. Don't worry about it. You
were just talking.

MARLENE: Uh, why don't you sit down—anywhere.
You hungry?

SPIN: Yeah. I'm hungry.

MARLENE: O K. I got some food. I'll make us some
food.

SPIN: Great. That's great.
She takes off her little hat, like a beret, and starts to
cook. She's pretty, doing that. Her eyes shine.
She's excited that I'm there, and that she's cooking, and
I'm watching her.
We eat. We eat roast chicken, and creamed spinach,
and potatoes browned in the pan grease in the oven.
We have pistachio nuts and bananas for dessert, and
drink sweet wine.
I walk over to the window. It's still snowing. City
lights blink on and off through the haze of snow. She
comes to the window and stands beside me. She takes
my hand.

MARLENE: I like the snow, but I'm glad we're not out there. There are people worse off than us tonight. Having a roof over your head is something.

SPIN: Yeah. Yeah, it is. I like it here.

MARLENE: My name's Marlene.

SPIN: I'm Spin.

MARLENE: What kinda name is that?

SPIN: You know, like how the world goes around.

MARLENE: That's a funny name to have.

SPIN: Maybe so.

MARLENE: Where you staying tonight, Spin? You got a place?

SPIN: In the park. I been sleeping in the park.

MARLENE: You can stay here. There's enough room for the two of us—until the landlady kicks us out.

(Quiet. MARLENE *and* SPIN *kiss.)*

MARLENE: One hundred, ninety-nine, ninety-eight, ninety-seven, ninety-six….THREE

(Music)

SPIN: Zig zag, and her face goes all Picasso.

(Dream Express sings and plays)

Come and Get Your Love (Milton Version)

Hey, *(Hey)* what's the matter with your head yeahhh

Hey, *(Hey)* what's the matter with your mind and your sign and a oooh ooh ooh

Hey, *(Hey)* nothing the matter with your head, baby, find it, come on and find it

Hey, with it baby cause you're find and you're mine and you look so divine

Come and get your love
Come and get your love
Come and get your love
Come and get your love

Hey, *(Hey)* what's the matter with your feel right, got to feel right baby

Hey, *(Hey)* it's your business if you want some, take some

Get it together baby

Come and get your love
Come and get your love
Come and get your love
Come and get your love
Come and get your love
Come and get your love
Come and get your love now
Come and get your love

Come and get your love
Come and get your love
Come and get your love
Come and get your love

Hey, *(Hey)* what's the matter with your head!

(Music ends.)

MARLENE: Once upon a time, Spin and me are cruising across Nevada at the midnight hour. In the vast desert between Frenchman's Cliff, a town made of wood, and Eureka, a town made of brick and steel—we run out of gas. Spin hauls out an empty can from the trunk.

SPIN: Saw an all-nite Sunoco a few miles back. Stay with the vehicle. No sense both of us walking miles in the nighttime. Gila monsters out there.

MARLENE: He starts to walk away. He stops, looks up at the sky.

SPIN: Hey, baby, those stars are cold.

MARLENE: Bye bye, Spin.
He's gone, and I lean back on the hood. Watch says
one ten in the A M. That light way out there... Zat a
firefly? Or a wandering soul? No room left in hell so
the damned are set loose in Nevada with their heads
forever on fire.
I'm thinking this sort of shit out there in the middle of
nowhere and the light comes closer, and I can see it's
not one light at all, but a circle of lights, hovering about
fifty feet off the ground. Uh oh. I get in the car, lock
the doors, and before I know it *he's* standing there in
the headlights. A small man in a white linen suit with
a Nehru collar. His black hair's painted on. He looks
like a young Peter Lorre at some fictional garden party.
Thin lips, and very frail somehow, as if a wind could
lift him and blow him gently away.
Then the headlights went out. All four locked doors
flew open and I fainted.
This next part is in very soft focus. I'm lying on my
back, and spidery fingers poke my body, my face.
I struggle. Then I feel a sharp pain in my belly, and
there's a smell like pomegranates.
Then I'm in a golden room and the being who
resembles Peter Lorre is sitting next to me on a sofa. He
sounds like Peter Lorre too.

SPIN: *(As Lorre alien)* I am from a far place. You call it
the Spiral Nebula in Ganymede. By the way, you bit
me.

MARLENE: I what?

SPIN: *(As alien)* Your child will be born under a distant
sun.

MARLENE: My what?

SPIN: *(As alien)* I am a...research person. You bit me,
Marlene.

MARLENE: I'm sorry. Oh God. You're gonna put me in a zoo in another galaxy.

SPIN: *(As alien)* Who told you that? It's a filthy lie, Marlene. I wouldn't hurt a girl like you. How could you even think such terrible thoughts.
Please. Show me your world.

MARLENE: Well, O K. I'm showing our world to this alien being. You come too.

(Sound of saucer take-off)

MARLENE: Bye bye, Briarpatch Lounge.

SPIN: *(As alien)* Briarpatch Lounge…hmmmm…

MARLENE: Look! That's the Grand Canyon!

SPIN: *(As alien)* The Grand Canyon…

MARLENE: Look, there's the Eiffel Tower!

SPIN: *(As alien)* La Tour Eiffel.

MARLENE: Look! The Lucky Dog Motel.

SPIN: *(As alien)* L'Auberge du Chien au Bonne Chance. Closer, Marlene.

MARLENE: A man is in Room Ten, lying on the bed. He's smoking a cigarette and looking at the ceiling. He's drunk and thoughtless.

SPIN: *(As alien)* Closer still, Marlene.

MARLENE: No, not completely thoughtless. He's thinking of a Daffy Duck cartoon he saw once on T V.

SPIN: *(As alien)* Le canard fou est tres amusant.

MARLENE: Why are you talking in French?

SPIN: *(As alien)* It's the language of love, Marlene. Lie back on my sofa. Close your eyes, and have the nicest little dream…

(Alien dream music under…)

MARLENE: Look. Girl at the wheel of a black Monte Carlo in a white T shirt, sun is shining like a Carribean lemon. Car radio's playing. She's pregnant, isn't she? She pulls off the road, down under the viaduct… gotta meet someone. *(Sings)* "Just walk away, Renee, you won't see me follow you back home…"

SPIN: Summer night along the lake road. Taking a walk. "Look honey. A falling star. Make a wish."

MARLENE: Parking lot of the shopping mall, and a three year old girl is running between the cars in a pink party dress. Mommmy! Mommmy! I wanna go inna Price-Chopper with Mommy.

SPIN: On the back lawn, lying on his belly in the grass, a boy's reading a comic book—*Crimson Claw Adventures—The Return of Doctor Death*. Wow. Far overhead floats a single white cloud.

MARLENE: There's a room in Milwaukee that faces Hannay street, and in that room a man watches T V. This T V is playing an old movie, black and white people from the dead time dance across the little screen in their gowns and tuxedos. Everyone in that dancehall of the dead is gone, dust and ashes in your mouth. A young girl's shoulders gleam in the party lights… "You want to dance with me?"

SPIN: She's sitting on the edge of the bathtub in a house in a Connecticut suburb. She's got a husband asleep in the bedroom, two kids already in college. She writes a note in lipstick on the mirror. Says I love you jinglebells. Then she swallows a handful of seconal and lies down on the tiles to rest…

MARLENE: Old man pulled over on the Interstate Parkway sitting in the driver's side door like a toddler with his pants wet, piss dripping down into his shoe. He needs a shave and his eyes are red with crying.

SPIN: "You don't worry about me, kids. My wife's gonna come get me. We live right over in Boynton Beach" —

MARLENE: Only his wife's been dead for ten years and Boynton Beach is three thousand miles away.

SPIN: "Come into this world bare ass, and when you go out you might have a suit on. That's the only difference."

MARLENE: And ain't that how we live...

(Alien dream music ends.)

MARLENE: Look! There's Nevada, with those cacti. There's my car!

SPIN: *(As alien)* Goodnight, Marlene. Au revoir.

(Sound of saucer take-off.)

MARLENE: And then the alien being and his ship were gone. I was lying on the sand alongside the vehicle, looking up at the cold stars.
You know, our world is the most beautiful of all the worlds god made. It has the most beautiful people in it. Why are so many of them weeping?

(Long beat)

SPIN: Amnesia. Long John the Doctor knows. Amnesia makes it hard to remember that we live in Paradise. And we're not talking about Diddy Wah Diddy, all painted up like rainbows, where the lemonade springs and the bluebird sings, up in the pearly clouds of love.

MARLENE: You know where it really is, baby. My little baby. The gate of heaven—it's right here, darlin', in the piss-stink hallways.
In shit.
I'm Marlene Milton, and this is my ex-husband, Spin—but that's just a label. You're riding through the night on the Dream Express. Spin's at the throttle, we lost

our airbrakes, and we're doing ninety down a twelve
percent grade. Hit it…

(Music)

(Dream Express sings and plays)

Do Ya Think I'm Sexy (Milton Version)

He sits alone, waiting for suggestions
She's so nervous, avoiding all the questions
His lips are dry, her heart is gently pounding
Don't you just know, exactly what they're thinking

If you want my body, and you think I'm sexy
Come on sugar tell me know
If you really need me,
Just reach out and touch me
Come on honey let me so, *(So me no, baby)*

He's acting shy, cause all the birds are singing
Two total strangers, lets spend the night together
Outside it's cold, it's misty, and it's raining
Give me a dime, so I can call my mother
He says I'm sorry, but I'm out of milk and coffee
Never mind that sugar. we can watch an early movie

And so we watched in amazement
As the miller told his tale
As her face at first just ghostly

Turned a whiter shad of pale
Doot doot doot etc…

(End music)

MARLENE: Thank you. babies. Thank you all so much.
You know, love is a Mystery. Capital M. It's a cracked
window in a strange hotel room, look out down the
alley to a violet streetlamp on the boulevard, down the
boulevard to the city line, climb halfway up a ragged
hillside over the highway, get your back against a tree
and wait. Light up a smoke and wait for something.

Love is in that waiting, little blue glow on the earth line
tells you it's day and the night has ended.

You're in the kitchen and the butter go sizzle in the
pan, and you pour in two eggs, and stir 'em around,
look over your shoulder and she got the little bunny's
head in her orange juice and she's laughing and
laughing.

Somebody just opens their blue eyes wide, and lets you
look inside.

Now is the hour of the dragon, that hour of the deep
night when our hearts are open. Sharing is caring. And
total sharing is total caring. We care about every one of
you. We wish you peace.

Have a last one——cause it's just about closing time.
And when you get home tonight, safe in bed——right
before you drift off to sleep, take a moment, and think
on Spin and me.

(A long silence)

You'll be back here tomorrow night. I know you will.
I asked the management to put a little "comeback" in
your drinks...

(SPIN shows a small bottle of liquid.)

SPIN: One drop is all it takes.

MARLENE: You know what the preacher and the
politician have to say? You can see that message on
your T V, in your newspaper, on the street—

SPIN: Them that hath shall be given some more, and
them that ain't got never shall get, world without end,
thus and forever, amen children.

MARLENE: You know what we say? Spin and me?

MARLENE & SPIN: No cover, no minimum.

SPIN: We giveth, and we ain't taking nothing away.
And please remember, boys and girls. If you do have
trouble in love, just singe the hair off a dead black

cat, and fill its mouth with lemon peel and melted red crayons.

MARLENE: Crayola.

SPIN: Wrap the body in tinfoil…

MARLENE: Alcoa.

SPIN: …and leave it where the one you desire is sure to pass it by.

MARLENE: Good night. Say your prayers. Pleasant dreams.

SPIN: Keep your nose clean, use the man inside, be kind to everyone. We're back at the Briarpatch tomorrow night. Join us. Meanwhile, enjoy the garden.

(Music)

SPIN: Lay down, my dear brother,
Won't you lay and take your rest,
Won't you lay your head down
On your Maker's breast.
Oh I love you
But the Good Lord loves you the best,
And I bid you goodnite, goodnite, goodnite

Lay down, my dear sister,
Won't you lay and take your rest
Won't you lay your head down
On your father's breast
Oh I love you,
But the Good Lord loves you the best
And I bid you goodnite, goodnite, goodnite

Lay down, my dear children
Won't you lay and take your rest,
Won't you lay your head down
Upon your mother's breast,
Oh we love you,
But the Good Lord loves you the best
And I bid you goodnite, goodnite, goodnite

And I bid you goodnite, goodnite, goodnite
Goodnite, goodnite, goodnite
Yeah I bid you goodnite, goodnite, goodnite
And I bid you goodnite, goodnite, goodnite

Goodnite, sleep tight, don't let the bedbugs bite.
Goodnite moon, goodnite brush, goodnite old lady,
whispering hush...

(End music. The phone rings. SPIN and MARLENE look at each other, then exit. The stage is empty except for their mikes, keyboard, etc. Phone continues ringing. Click of a connection)

WOLFIE: *(On phone)* Gotcha! Heh heh. *(Pause)* It's your Uncle Wolfie, calling you from nowhere. Spin? You there? *(Pause)* Maybe they're asleep. It's late.
"Lay down, my dear children, won't you lay and take your rest, Lay your head on your Uncle Wolfie's breast..."
Marlene? You there? *(Pause)* I'd drag my balls across broken...heh heh heh. What the hell. I'll be in touch.

(Click, as the phone goes dead)

(Encore. The Dream Express return to the stage.)

SPIN: Here's a little cupcake to take home with you.

(Music)

(Dream Express sings and plays)

I Think We're Alone Now (Milton Version)

Children behave,
That's what they say when we're together
And watch how you play,
They don't understand
And so we're running just as fast as we can
Holding on to one another's hand Trying to get away
into the night And then you put your arms around me
as we tumble to the ground and then you say

I think we're alone now
There doesn't seem to be anyone around
I think we're alone now
The beating of our hearts is the only sound

Look at the way
We gotta hide what we're doing Cause what would
they say
If they ever knew
And so we're running just as fast as we can
Holding on to one another's hand Trying to get away
into the night And then you put your arms around me
as we tumble to the ground and then you say

I think we're alone now

There doesn't seem to be anyone around
I think we're alone now
The beating of our hearts is the only sound
Ahhhhhhhhh Ahhhhhhhhhh
Ahhhhhhhhh Ahhhhhhhhhh

And so we watched in amazement
As the miller told his tale
As her face at first just ghostly
Turned a whiter shade of pale
Doot doot doot etc…

THANK YOU!

(And out)

(Train sound. as MARLENE *and Spin exit)*

END OF SET 1

ADDITIONAL SONGS & STORIES

What follows here are all the songs and stories created after SET 1, during the years the show was performed. That these scenes are relegated to this "Additional Songs and Stories" section is in no way a comment on their quality. They are among the best of the DREAM EXPRESS. Please take this material as of equal weight with SET 1, and shuffle the cards, creating the show that feels right for the time, the place, and the creative team.

Here are two lists that might help: the set list for Set 1, and a list of all the additional material in the order given here, which is roughly the order of their creation. Songs are labelled according to their source: original, cover, traditional, or dream version, which is a cover song with changed lyrics.

If you think of creating a version of THE DREAM EXPRESS as deciding on a list of songs and stories for a band, with highs amd ;pws, and alternating rhythms, whatever dramatic builds emerge—you won't be off the mark.

SET 1

Intro
Let's Get Physical (Dream version)
Town Well (original)
Long John the Doctor
Pina Colada Song (Dream version)
Spin Almost Dies
Spin's riff
Hitch-hiker
Wear Your Love Like Heaven (Dream version)
Uncle Wolfie calls
Fuck You, I'm a Millionaire (original)
Intermission talk
Charlie (original)
The Other Dream Express
Changes (cover)
How They Met (With Walk Away Renee (cover)
Come And Get Your Love (cover)
Alien Abduction
Amnesia
Do Ya Think I'm Sexy (cover version)
Love is a Mystery
I Bid You Goodnight (traditional)
Uncle Wolfie Calls again
Encore—I Think We're Alone Now (cover)

ADDITIONAL SONGS & STORIES
(Numbered as follows)

1. Tumbleweed Song (original)
2. Dead Boys Don't Cry (original, with intro)
3. Marlene and the Devil (original)
4. Are You Ready? (traditional hymn)
5. Death of Uncle Wolfie and He Was a Friend of Mine (traditional)
6. New Orleans arrest and trial and House of the Rising Sun (traditional)
7. Invisible Man
8. Woman and the Devil by the Railroad track
9. Dream Express Song (original)
10. Pedro's Full Moon Tavern
11. Carry Me (A K A Engineer Bill-cover w/ additional material)
12. Marlene and the chicken
13. Tiny Topsy
14. New High Water Blues (original)
15. Dairy Queen
16. Sexy Spin and Treat Her Like a Lady (cover)
17. Roger Harvey's Brain and I Get Drunk on Christmas (original song, for the holidays only)
18. Alastair Sim Christmas Carol sequence (for the holidays only)
19. It's All Right Now (Dream version)
20. To introduce backup singers, if they appear

1.

MARLENE & SPIN: *(Sing)*
Down in the west, down west
We weeds dance
Down west, down in the west
Along the Milky Way.

Down west, down west
We weeds dance
Down west, down in the west
Along the Milky Way.

MARLENE: The Tumbleweed song.

SPIN: I learned that one from a big daddy weed hung
up on a fence outside Las Cruces. I saved his life.

2.

SPIN: We have something special for you this evening,
an old number that's forever new. This tune was our
first waxing on Vee-Jay cut of Chicago, hit the charts
with a bullet, heavy regional airplay, mostly in the corn
belt, back when we were known as

MARLENE & SPIN: "Little Marlene and the Miltones."

MARLENE: It peaked at number 37 in Billboard Midwest
Edition and I dropped out of sixth grade to begin my
show business career. We played the Green Mill, Tri-
City Motor Lodge, did the Fox Paramount on the same
bill with Tiny Topsy and her Big Girl Revue.
Those big girls from the South Side gave me styling
tips and I showed them the little pink ball in the
Darvon capsule. You remember the little pink ball…

(Music)

MARLENE: I may look like I was born yesterday, but I was up all night.

MARLENE & SPIN: *(Sing and play)*

Dead Boys Don't Cry

Johnny was a he-man
He was playing by the pool
Workin' on a suntan
Actin' like a fool
Dancin' on the diving board
He fell down on his head
Now his brains are chlorinated
And the rest of Johnny's dead

I hate to tell a lie
I found another guy
But Johnny doesn't have to know
'Cause Johnny's in the sky

(Chorus)

Dead boys don't cry
Dead boys don't cry
Oh me oh my
Dead boys—they don't cry

Bobby was a scientist
He liked my D N A
I liked his logarithm
He could tabulate all day
He was messin' with some molecules
While playin' in the lab
Now his brains are in the ozone
And the rest is on a slab

I hate to tell a lie
I found another guy
But Bobby doesn't have to know
'Cause Bobby's in the sky

(Chorus)

Tommy was a warrior
He made me shine his boots
He wore a needle in his nose
And didn't dye his roots
He got into a rumble
At a cockfight in Ocala
Now his brains are in a trashcan
But his soul's gone to Valhalla

I hate to tell a lie
I found another guy
But Tommy doesn't have to know
'Cause Tommy's in the sky

(Chorus)

3.

SPIN: It's 9:15. Do you know where your daughters are?
Have you read them the Mann Act?

(Music)

MARLENE: *(With* SPIN. *Sings and plays)*
This is about me and the Devil…a love story. The
devil is a complicated subject, as I'm sure some of you
know. I'll tell you he's all he's cracked up to be. You
walk in on a place he's been and you know it by his
teethmarks, and his smell. But he's got a sweet side too.

SPIN: Thank you, baby.

MARLENE: Suffice it to say, it was one of the many
times I'd climbed out the window, thirteen years old
and blue sparkle polish on all twenty nails, hit the road
out of town, and the Devil himself pulled over in a '66
El Dorado and we liked each other right away. He was
scary, and I liked to be scared. Perfect. We drove and
stopped, and drove and stopped, and drove and when
you're a wild child who can't stay still you don't notice
the road has gotten nasty and the old man beside you

with horns on his head is your actual boyfriend, and I
don't use the word lightly.

We landed at a little hotel clinging to a cliff
overlooking the Mexican Pacific where the yellow sun
shined all day long but me and my boyfriend never
saw it. We stayed in and ate sweet leilani cakes and he
showed me secret devil stuff in our cool room with the
blinds down. And the Devil would say…

SPIN: "You're not scared of nothing, are you?"

MARLENE: And I'd say "No, I'm not," and then he'd
sing me a song:

MARLENE & SPIN: "Marlene, Marlene, you're the
prettiest thing I've ever seen
I'm a mean old Devil and I'm full of spleen,
But you make me good and you make me clean,
Marlene."

MARLENE: I'd say "I don't want you good, I don't want
you clean," and he'd laugh. And time turned inside
out, like it does in these situations and we got so pale
you could see right through us, like you do in these
situations. Then one night I had a dark dream where
the edges of everything looked like cut glass. You
know those kind of dreams? I woke up in the black
black foreign land far from home night and shook
the devil's shoulder. "Hey, Devil, wake up sweetie.
Guess what? I'm scared." My boyfriend rolled over
and looked at me hard and long and he saw that I was
shivering, and I was a little girl. I was his meat now.

SPIN: Pass the ketchup.

MARLENE: He got out of bed and found a dime for the
phone.

SPIN: Wait here, little darling, I gotta make a call.

MARLENE: Two hours later I looked out the window to
see my Grandma Gussie get out of her old blue Valiant.

She looked tough and dusty and tired. The Devil walked over to her. He leaned down and kissed her on the cheek. She looked up at him and sighed "You haven't changed a bit."

SPIN: Thank you, baby.

MARLENE: In the car I lay in the back seat and cried all the way home. Grandma Gussie didn't yell at me and she didn't say nothing nice. She just drove and drank bad coffee and drove and smoked PallMalls and drove and drank bad coffee and drove, and smoked PallMalls and drove.

(End music)

4.

(Music begins.)

MARLENE & SPIN: *(Sing and play)*

Are You Ready

Are you ready
For your new home in the sky
Think your luck will finally turn around
The minute that you die
And all those prophets
Who profit from your fears
Will they stand and hold your hand
When the end is finally near?

Are you ready
To claim your great reward?
Climb those shiny stairs
And shake hands with your Lord
And look down on those poor sinners such as I
Who missed our chance to be redeemed
Will your laughter drown our cries?

Are you ready
To leave this sinful world
Read your name
When that great scroll is unfurled
And if Jesus calls you home
When that angel trumpet sounds
Won't you just leave me alone
When I'm six feet underground.

Are you ready?

(End music)

5.

MARLENE: Some of you out there already know this, but the Dream Express is temporarily without a booking agent.
Uncle Wolfie, our longtime manager, made a last run. The high tide left his story on the beach, and it's worth the telling.
Tell it, baby.

SPIN: Wolfie meets an Italian contessa in a bar in Pasadena.

MARLENE: Giovanna.

SPIN: She offers to give her ageing loverman an apartment she owns in Citta di Castello, small town in Italy, near Perugia.

MARLENE: Stay as long as you like.

SPIN: She says. Wolfie sees the EXIT sign light up. In his mind he steps into a landscape out of Botticelli, leaving behind all the bullshit, frustration, injustice, and painful garbage of his American life. He shoves his clothes in a bag, empties his pathetic bank account, and heads for the airport. He arrives in Citta di Castello to find that the address she'd given him doesn't exist.

MARLENE: *Mi dispiace…*

SPIN: No one knows her. He tries Pasadena, and Giovanna's phone is disconnected. Maybe the bitch was having him on—a joke. Maybe she was an agent of that dark god who gives men one more chance than they deserve. Wolfie wasn't giving up on La Vita Nuova. He tosses the contessa's key in a trash can, and checks into the Albergo del Sole, a dump on Via Parini, an alley behind the cathedral. He pays for a month, so he won't be tempted to drink up the rent. They give him a top floor room, small and neat, like a child's. Uncle Wolfie spends his days in a cafe, Il Fiore on Via Bufalini, International Herald Tribune, Pall Malls, and watch the girls go by. He makes one beer last most of the day, and no one bothers him. His clothes become filthy, and he lets his beard grow.

He eats dinner in a cheap Chinese place.

MARLENE: Ristorante Hong Kong.

SPIN: Most nights he's the only customer. He feels at home, knowing that these silent impassive people serving him are also refugees from some other place, some other time.

(Music)

SPIN: Empty street at dawn, Wolfie can't sleep, wheeze in the chest like a busted tire pump, grins at some passing schoolgirls coming around the corner, makes for Il Fiore, *Una birra, signorina…* He's got the shakes already, takes out his cell, makes a call to the states— This is your Uncle Wolfe calling you from paradise, where the crows circle over the olive trees…I'll be in touch…

That evening he goes to the Cinema Eden where they show movies from the sixties. During *Per Un Pugno Di Dollari* he begins coughing uncontrollably, and then he vomits over the seats, and over himself. He lies there

in the aisle, one leg twitching, as Clint strides across
the screen. An usher throws Uncle Wolfie out into the
street.

(Music fades.)

MARLENE: He'd been gone about three months, when
there was a knock on our door at the Red Robin
Motorlodge outside of Spokane.

SPIN: "I'm the Nightman. Somebody's calling you from
Italy. You can take it in the office."

MARLENE: It was a Doctor Lorenzo from the local
hospital. A blood vessel burst inside Wolfie's head. His
liver was shot, and his lungs had filled with fluid. They
couldn't do anything for him. He died on Christmas
eve. No doubt the fucking church bells were ringing.

SPIN: Doctor Lorenzo spoke good English. Signor
Wolfie wanted you to know, he said. When he knew he
wouldn't make it, he wanted you to know. He said to
remind you— "Make 'em laugh, make 'em cry, make
'em kiss ten bucks goodbye." *Buona sera.* Good night.

MARLENE: So you see, Uncle Wolfie himself, the pied
piper, God's own cowboy, a gentleman of rare spark,
died alone in the hilltown of Citta di Castello, a long
ways from home, and lies uncomforted in the cold
Italian earth. Live while you can, babies. Old news, but
true.

MARLENE & SPIN: *(Sing and play)*

He was a Friend of Mine

He was a friend of mine
He was a friend of mine
Never had no money, to pay for his fine
He was a friend of mine

He died on the road
He died on the road

Never had no money, to pay his room and board
He was a friend of mine

He never done no wrong
He never done no wrong
He was just a poor boy, a long ways from home
He was a friend of mine

I stole away and cried
I stole away and cried
Never had no money, and I can't be satisfied
He was a friend of mine

He was a friend of mine
He was a friend of mine
When I hear his name,
I just can't keep from crying
He was a friend of mine

6.

MARLENE: After Uncle Wolfie's exit from this vale
of tears, Spin and me found ourselves cut loose in
the backside of New Orleans, starved, stalled, and
stranded. Our coffee was getting weak. Unfortunately,
I met with certain legal difficulties. In fact, I was
looking at 3 to 5.
Spin signed up for a correspondence course from the
Legal Eagle School of Law.
Spin takes out a book, the correspondence course.

SPIN: Page 37, lesson 4. When all else fails, sprinkle
courtroom with a liberal dose of Other Attorney
Be Stupid powder. *(He takes out the powder.)* Other
Attorney Be Stupid Powder, guaranteed to fog the
mind of opposing counsel, and help your client win
big!
(SPIN sprinkles the powder liberally.)

SPIN: *Habeas corpus. Manet omnes una nox. Quo animoso,* baby!

MARLENE: Spin represented me in court to great effect.

(Music)

*(*MARLENE *sings* House of the Rising Sun *under what follows.)*

SPIN: Will the defendant please take the stand.

MARLENE: Hi, your honor.

SPIN: Your honor, the charge of solicitation is bullshit.

MARLENE: I like your outfit, your honor.

SPIN: It's a personal insult that a man of your obvious refinement can suggest that Marlene could view love as a commercial enterprise.

MARLENE: Take that mattress off your back, girls!

SPIN: Why, she doesn't even know where the Grand Hyatt is.

MARLENE: Hey sugar, where's the Grand Hyatt?

SPIN: Your majesty, may I approach the bench? At the time in question Marlene was laid up in bed with the croup. The testimony of the chef at the Bien Ville Grille is a tissue of lies, and his Oysters Rockefeller are improperly seasoned. Your honor, I found it necessary to disgorge the offending mollusks upon the dining room carpet in full view of the afternoon clientele while Miss Milton submitted herself to the humiliation of a full body cavity search and a naked lie detector test, both of which she passed with flying colors. *(Pointing at* MARLENE*)*
Your honor, the face of an angel.

MARLENE: (House of the Rising Sun*)*
...mothers tell your children
Not to do what I have done

And spend your life in pain and misery
In the house of the rising sun

(Music ends.)

SPIN: Case dismissed!

MARLENE: Not guilty.

SPIN: The law is a diseased harlot.

7.

(Sound of wind)

SPIN: Somewhere in the midlands

(More wind)

SPIN: At last, an inn. The Slaughtered Lamb.

(Wind. knocking)

MARLENE: Who could that be in this 'orrible blizzard?

(More knocking. Door opens. Wind)

MARLENE: Yes?

SPIN: I want a room and a fire.

MARLENE: Of course, sir. Millie!

SPIN: A private sitting room.

MARLENE: Millie, show this gentleman to the private sitting room. Sir, your face. It's covered in bandages.

SPIN: I've had a serious accident. It disfigured me.

MARLENE: Just your face, sir, or your willy, and your bum, and…

SPIN: I came here for quiet and secrecy. It's life or death that I be left alone. And bring me some food.

MARLENE: It's leg of mutton this evening sir. With mustard. Nothing like a bit of tasty mustard.

SPIN: Shut up, you ignorant bitch!

Act II.

There must be a way back. God knows there's a way back! The formula! I must remember.

(He takes out a pencil on a string, moving it in the air to indicate that he's invisible, and writing.)

MARLENE: Your mustard, sir. It's always nice to have a bit of tasty…AHHHH!!

(SPIN swings the pencil wildly.)

SPIN: A few chemicals mixed together, and flesh and bone just fade away. Any invisible man can rule the world. Nobody will see him come, nobody will see him go!

MARLENE: Ahhh! I'm calling the constable!

SPIN: Shut up, you fool or I'll…

MARLENE: Constable Willie!

SPIN: Ah! The window!

(He tosses the pencil away, and thus the invisible man and his visible pencil go out through an invisible window.)

8.

SPIN: Picture this.

MARLENE: In your mind, Charlie.

SPIN: *(With* MARLENE*)* The middle of nowhere.
At high noon on a hot summer day, a woman is standing by the side of a railroad track with a sack full of demons.
Up comes the Devil.
"I believe you have some friends of mind in that big bag of yours."

MARLENE: That's right! I whupped these fuckers late last night and I'm waiting for the 12:15 out of Dunbar to come along so I can squash them flat.

SPIN: I could stop you.

MARLENE: You could try. But then I'd kick your ass and throw you in this big bag too.

SPIN: Oh, I hate the rough stuff. Instead, let me tell you a story. Once upon a…
He proceeds to tell a tale so immediately boring that the woman falls asleep right there standing up. And before she knows what's what, she dreams she is standing by the side of a railroad track at high noon on a hot summer day with a sack full of demons.
Along comes the 12:15 out of Dunbar big and black and belching steam.
The woman throws the bag onto the tracks in front of that train and those demons inside wiggle and scream until—pow! —the locomotive smacks them flat and rumbles past. The woman sees the smashed remains of her demon bag on the tracks, the rails smoking with infernal gore. And as a smile lights her face, she is awakened by the sound of the real world 12:15 whooshing by.

(Train sound)

SPIN: No sign of her sack anywhere. Just the buzzing of insects in the quivering heat. And a note in her hand that reads, "I win. Your boyfriend, the Devil."

MARLENE: Damn: Old Scratch tricked me. That train was just a dream. Wait till I tell Spin.

9.

(Music)

MARLENE & SPIN: *(Sing and play)*

Dream Express Song

A young man seeking wisdom
Climbs a mountain in Tibet
In a cave he finds a wise man
Who bums a cigarette
The young man asks the wise man
"What's the secret to success?"
The wise man puffs and smiles and says
"Catch the Dream Express."

In the lobby of a motel
Off an access road
A salesman with his samples
Sees the nightclerk's head implode
In his room he stares at nothing
His life's an awful mess
A brochure on the nightstand reads "Catch the Dream
Express."

A crackhead high on cocaine
Her body craving more
Picks a house on Elm Street
Breaks in through the back door
She finds an old guy giving
His flannel pants a press
She pulls a gun, he says "Don't Shoot!
Catch the Dream Express."

If your life's spent merely waiting
For the reapers grim caress
If you know you didn't do it
But you're ready to confess
If you wake up on some trestle
In your ex-wife's cocktail dress

Head downtown, catch a ride
On the Dream Express

10.

(Mexican music)

MARLENE: Pedro's Full Moon Tavern. Buenos
Noches… Ayeeeah!

(Music fades under.)

SPIN: You say we tried—and it's over. Fuck we tried. I
tried. It's only over for you.

MARLENE: What? You say something to me?

SPIN: Sorry. I'm sorry. I was talking to…

MARLENE: There's no one else here, Jim. Just us.
You ought to come back here rodeo time, Jim. They got
some bulls here like you've never seen. Like Crooked
Nose. Only got one horn, but he's a smart son-of-a-
bitch. Once you come out of the chute enough times,
you don't take the fake no more.
What kind of work you do?

SPIN: I rent space. Underground. Long term.

MARLENE: You got a cemetery or something, Jim?

SPIN: Storage. Climate controlled. One thousand
feet down in solid rock. Corporations are my main
customers. They store data.

MARLENE: Data? That's some kind of job you got
yourself, Jim.

SPIN: One guy, last week, he wanted this C D he
recorded to still be available when the souls rise up out
off their graves. At the apocalypse. The end of da…

MARLENE: I know what the fucking word means.

SPIN: His contract said the only people who could retrieve this C D were himself, or Jesus Christ. Well, goodnight, Miss...

MARLENE: Don't go yet. We're just starting to have fun.

SPIN: *(Looks at his watch)* It's 1:09 in the A M. I'm tired.

MARLENE: That's no excuse. I was at work at six this morning. That's when the dayshift punches in. Where you staying?

SPIN: Thunderbird Lodge. Right across the road.

MARLENE: Convenient. Hey, what's that tattoo you got on your arm?

SPIN: A name. Alberta.

MARLENE: Al what?

SPIN: Berta.

MARLENE: Who the fuck is Alberta?

SPIN: Girl I met when I was in the Coast Guard. Her father was my lieutenant. Lost track of her until last month, some guy told me she burned to death in a forest fire. Twenty years ago. So I'm carrying around somebody's name on my arm for the rest of my life. Girl who isn't even around anymore.

MARLENE: Once the bullet leaves the barrel, you can't call it back. Not ever. If you been through some difficult shit, you *know*. Am I right here, Jim.

SPIN: Oh, yeah.

MARLENE: The thing I was involved in wasn't working out, I should've known, but I'm just a little, well, hopeful. If that's the word. But after that shit in the parking lot of the goddamn Price Chopper with my kid in the back seat hearing every word, I understood, with perfect clarity, that some people are not out for your best interests. Okay, I'll try something else, you know what I'm saying? Well, what do you do? And it's like this boy with the missing finger keeps popping into my head.

SPIN: Missing finger?

MARLENE: Boy I knew in High School. He grew up dirt poor, so they had to eat turtle meat. Snapper. He picked up a big one outta the mud, and the bastard bit off the index finger of his left hand.

(SPIN *demonstrates.)*

SPIN: Like this?

MARLENE: Yeah. It's gotten weird lately, this missing finger shit.
What is it, like midnight'

SPIN: *(Looks at watch)* It's 1:09 in the A M.

MARLENE: Oh man, I keep thinking I'm supposed to be someplace, but I don't know where. You gonna make love to me, or do I have to find somebody else?

(A long silence. A dog howls in the distance.)

MARLENE: Why the fuck is it so quiet?

SPIN: The apocalypse. Happened right outside, while we were talking.

MARLENE: Shit, we missed it, Jim. The rain of fire, the beast, the pale horse..

SPIN: Only the two of us were saved.

MARLENE: Great fucking choice. Lemme just peek outside the window, make sure everything's still there…

(MARLENE goes over to the window, is about to pull aside the curtain and look out. SPIN's voice stops her.)

SPIN: Don't look.

MARLENE: O K. I won't look.
What time you got?

SPIN: 1:09 in the A M.

MARLENE: Well, Jim, it's still a long ways till morning.

SPIN: The morning will come. Not even the Devil can stop the sunrise.

11.

(Music)

MARLENE & SPIN: *(Sing and play)*

Carry Me (Engineer Bill)

MARLENE: Won't you carry me
In troubling times
Won't you fill my sails
Won't you blow my mind
Put me on the path
Of a railroad car
Won't you make me laugh
About the way things are.

Won't you carry me
Through my soul's dark night
Won't you shine my way
With your big head light
Won't you lift me up
When I shiver and shake
Won't you change my lock
Won't you gimme a break
Gimme all your love
Gimme all your love
Gimme all your love

Won't you carry me
Won't you try to save me
Be my sugar daddy
Be my honey baby
Won't you be my lover

Be my loyal fan
Be my heavenly mother
Be my holy man

Won't you pick me up
In your one-eyed ford
Won't you drive me home
Like a good little lord
Won't you sing me to sleep
Won't you star in my dreams
Won't you dig me deep
Won't you do these things
Gimme all your love
Gimme all your love
Gimme all your love

SPIN: I'm not in the data storage business. Not
anymore. They fired me. My briefcase is filled with
mud. My suit hangs off my body in shreds. My skin
is cracked, oozing blood. I'm standing out here, in the
middle of a black field, a scarecrow. The crops have
rotted away. Behind me, the Thunderbird Lodge is in
flames. I am a brother to dragons, a companion to owls.
I want you. I want you. I want you.
I'm gone.

MARLENE: Won't you carry me
Be my voodoo child
Rock me in your cradle
When the ride gets wild
Be my black cat bone
Be my holy grail
Call me on the phone
Get me out of this jail

Won't you throw me a kiss
Won't you send me a sign
Be my Engineer Bill
To the end of the line
Won't you kill my heart

Be my virgin king
You're all that I got
Will you do these things
Gimme all your love
Gimme all your love
Gimme all your love

SPIN: I want you. I want you. I want you.
I'm gone.

(Music ends.)

12.

MARLENE: We had three nights at the Ramada in
downtown Flagstaff and we're on I-40, heading west.
It's late. Spin keeps dozing off at the wheel, having
little two second dreams, and then he has one for three
seconds...

SPIN: I'm in this S R O in Kansas City with Ingrid
Bergman. She's a nurse, this time, and she's peeling a
white stocking off one perfect thigh, and...

MARLENE: So we crash into a billboard. The front end's
fucked, but one headlight works, and we can move.
I take the wheel and we limp into Peach Springs and
check into this motel. T V next door is playing some
movie, volume way up, like the people watching are
almost dead. A man keeps saying...

SPIN: There must be a way back. God knows there's a
way back.

MARLENE: I can't sleep. I go outside, have a cigarette in
front of the motel. Then this bus pulls up right across
the highway. It's shining, like someone just polished
the metal. Glowing. Must be a hundred people pile out,
all Mexicans-old people in white shirts and pants with
straw hats, barefoot. And young families. They walk
around a bit, stretch their legs. A few of the men piss in

the grass by the roadside. One little kid has a chicken on a leash- a dirty piece of string. He walks across the highway right over to me, points to the chicken and holds out his hand. I give him a buck, and he gives me the end of the string.

MARLENE & SPIN: *(Sing)*
Take the end of this golden string
And wind it into a ball
It will lead you in to Heaven's Gate
Built in Jerusalem's wall

MARLENE: The Mexicans get back in the bus, pull away. The chicken squawks. I can still hear the TV through an open window.

SPIN: There must be a way back. God knows there's a way back.

MARLENE: I let go of the string. Everything else on earth is still, except for my chicken, runs off down the white line letting out little frightened squawks, like a madman. I go back inside. A big green moth buzzes against the window screen.
What the fuck am I doing here?

13.

MARLENE: Christmas eve, 1966. I'm twelve years old, and I'm on the road with Tiny Topsy and her Big Girl Revue. Tiny Topsy was five foot three in her stocking feet, weighed about three seventy-five, and was the greatest blues singer I've ever heard.
Picture this, in your mind. Topsy is lying in bed in the Empire Hotel like a beached whale. Her breath is coming hard. I can hear it, a low wheeze back in her throat. I'm sitting on the end of her bed, and we're playing five card stud for small change. I got a queen in the hole, and I toss in a quarter. Its snowing outside,

and the radio is tuned to a jazz station out of Chicago,
and Chet Baker is singing "Ghost of a Chance," and
Topsy says to me, That boy must have really got his
heart broke. Then she tosses down her cards, looks
me over, and says Marlene honey, little thing like you
needs a man who knows how to make money, not
some joker spend the afternoon in front of Nu Way
Liquors. And you need protection. Get a .38 so he
won't keep coming after you shoot him. And do me a
favor, honey. Take this tenspot, bring it down to the
desk, tell 'em to send Leon out to Popeye's for a bucket
of chicken and a bottle of beer. Say for Miss Topsy in
405.
I said, Yes, ma'am.
And Topsy laughs and says, I'll yes ma'am your ass.
You know something, Little Marlene? Some of these
nights, they just go on and on, like the clock stopped
ticking. Open those curtains so I can see the snow
falling. Then get outta here and do my business.

14.

MARLENE: Here's a little something for the people of
New Orleans, Queen City of the South, pearl of the
Mississippi—a song for the dead, and the living. New
High Water Blues…

(Music)

MARLENE & SPIN:
Rampart and Canal Street, down to Lake Ponchartrain
All muddy river, and the howl of the hurricane
Black clouds rolling, they cover up the sun
Momma and Poppa, they got no place to run
High water rising, oooh oooh ooh oooooo
High water all around.

My man's on the housetop, he begins to pray
Lord have mercy, don't take my life away

Hard times and sorrow is all high water brings
All you little children, better wear your water wings
High water rising, oooh ooooh ooh oooooo
High water all around

Two old ladies lying in bed,
One turned to the other and the other one said
Water in the alley is six feet high
Nobody cares if we live or die
High water rising, oooh oooh ooh oooooo
High water rising ooooh ooo oooooo

MARLENE: Thank you.

SPIN: *Laissez les bon temps roulez…*

15.

(New music under…)

SPIN: Somewhere in Virginia… Ah. A Dairy Queen.

MARLENE: You can't keep standing in front of the window not saying nothing. You been there ten minutes. You stand there, you're supposed to order something.

SPIN: Hot dog, and a coffee. *(Long beat)*
Don't you have to tell someone?

MARLENE: Tell someone what?

SPIN: About my hot dog.

MARLENE: He heard you.

SPIN: Who?

MARLENE: Felix. He hears everything. You know what he told me? He says, I hear all things in heaven and earth. I even hear the damned, whispering in hell.

SPIN: He's crazy.

MARLENE: You think so?

SPIN: What's he do back there?

MARLENE: He cooks.

SPIN: When he's not cooking.

MARLENE: I don't know. Nothing.

SPIN: What's he look like, Felix?

MARLENE: He's thin, you can see his bones. Pale.
Always smiling. His hair's white. Smokes those
Swisher Sweets, smells like dope. He sings a little song
while he works. You know what he told me? He told
me he didn't love anybody. Not anymore. That he was
done with people.

SPIN: Mister Felix got himself a negative attitude.

MARLENE: What's your name?

SPIN: Bob.

MARLENE: What kind of work you do, Bob?

SPIN: I'm a sales agent, like yourself.

MARLENE: Everybody selling something.

SPIN: My company provides secure underground
storage. We handle data for corporations.

MARLENE: You like doing that, selling storage?

SPIN: Why you have that wire screen across the
window?

MARLENE: Keeps out the flies.

SPIN: Slide it back so I can kiss you.

MARLENE: I'm not gonna do that.

SPIN: You like the mountains?

MARLENE: What are you talking about?

SPIN: You know. Scenery.

MARLENE: Do I like scenery?

SPIN: I know a place by a waterfall. We could take a ride up there tomorrow.

MARLENE: Tomorrow I got a parent-teacher thing. At my daughter's school.

SPIN: You married?

MARLENE: Not anymore.

SPIN: Where's my hotdog and coffee?

MARLENE: Felix? FELIX?
You married?

SPIN: Five years. My wife's in prison. Passing bad checks. Eileen's always doing some criminal shit.

MARLENE: Felix! Hot dog! FELIX!
'Scuse me just a sec.

(MARLENE *exits.*)

(MARLENE *returns.*)

SPIN: You O K?

MARLENE: Felix was standing in his apron by the fryolator, a batch of fries scattered over the floor at his feet. He looked at me. His eyes were pearls. Then he floated up and out the window. Up into the sky.
Felix is gone.

SPIN: Is this a joke?

MARLENE: Do I sound like I'm joking?

SPIN: Shouldn't we call someone?

MARLENE: What's the difference who the fuck we call.

SPIN: You want to take that ride now? Up to the mountains. By the waterfall.

MARLENE: I'm not gonna do that. I'm closing up. I gotta go home.

16.

MARLENE: Thank you, babies. Thank you so much. We are the Dream Express, and we're gonna turn this boat around with a little something for the ladies.

I've seen you out there, sweetheart, right under the streetlight, hair all tangled and feelin' like God's own fool. I've been there. I even know the motto you got stuck up on the fridge: "Live fast…learn slow."

Now girls, a private session, you heard me right, a completely private session with the love doctor himself, a.k.a Spin Milton, is now available. Blue Lantern Motor Lodge, out on the Beeline Highway. Convenient, right?

Now ladies, I know you've been thinking about getting next to Spin ever since we walked out here. The girls all want him, and the boys all want to know his secret. Is it his ass-pocket full of money? His '55 two-tone Chevy BelAir?

SPIN: Fluid drive.

MARLENE: That mojo hand he got in the swamp outside of Tuscaloosa?

SPIN: Come to Damballah.

MARLENE: Is it a secret of his anatomy?

(Music begins.)

MARLENE: Empire Hotel

SPIN: Room 701. Right behind the eight ball.

MARLENE: I'm at my sister's in Tahoe when you get straight

Treat Her Like A Lady

(BACKUP GIRLS *onstage.*)

MARLENE & SPIN: *(Sing)*
All my friends had to ask me

Somethin' they didn't understand-a
How I get all the women
In the palms of my hand, now
And I told them, treat her like a lad-ay
(You got-to, got-to treat her like)
Um-hum all the best you can do
(Treat her like, you got-to, got-to treat her like)
You got to treat her like a lad-ay, she give into you
Ah-hum now who can see, you know what I mean?
I know you heard (treat her right)
That a woman (got-ta treat her right)
Will soon take advantage (treat her right) of you
(Got-ta treat her right)
Let me tell you (treat her right)
My friend (got-ta treat her right)
There just ain't no (treat her right) subsititute-ta
(Got-ta treat her right)
You oughta treat her like a lad-ay
(You got-ta, got-ta treat her like)
Um-hum, all (treat her like) the best you can do
(You got-ta, got-ta treat her like)
You got-ta treat her like a lad-ay
She give into you, ah-hum
Now who can see? you know what I mean
Oh, you've got to love her (love her)
Tease her (tease her)
But most of all you've got-ta please her
(Please her)
You've got-ta hold her (hold her)
Now an want her (Want her)
And make her feel you'll always need her
(Need her)
You know a woman (woman)
Is sentimental (woman)
And so easy (woman) to upset (woman)
So make her feel (feel)
That she's for real (real)

An she give you happiness
Whoa-oh-oh
Strange (treat her like) as it seems-a
(You got-ta treat her like)
You know you can't (treat her like) a woman mean
(Got-ta treat her like)
So my friends, now there you have it
It's the easy simple way
Now if you fail, uh, ta do this
Don't blame her if she looks my way-a
Cause I'm gonna a
Treat her like a lad-ay
(You got-ta, got-ta treat her like)
Um-hum, so affec (treat her like) tionately
(You got-ta, got-ta treat her like)
I'm gonna treat her like a lad-ay
She give into me, uh-huh
Now who can see?
You know what I mean
Oh you gotta a treat her like a lad-ay
(You got-ta, got-ta treat her like)
Um-hum, all the best you can do
(You got-ta, got-ta treat her like)
You got-ta treat her like a lad-ay
She give into you...

(End music. BACKUP GIRLS *offstage)*

SPIN: I'm also gonna lay on you gentlemen out
there, for one green dollar and one thin dime, my
instructional video...

MARLENE: *(Holding up V H S tape, clearly labelled)* "How
Does He Do It?"

SPIN: ...with a six months supply of goofer dust, and a
fingerbone of Saint Genevieve on a golden chain.

MARLENE: 22 Karat.

MARLENE & SPIN: *(Eastern European accent)* We make your dreams come true.

17.

(Strange science music)

(SPIN places a jar containing a brain in liquid on the electronic keyboard. He connects his mike to the brainjar with alligator clips. He talks into his mike to the brain as MARLENE does calculations on a large pad of paper.)

SPIN: Roger. Roger Harvey. Since your fatal accident I have kept your brain alive in this jar for five months now. I realize that everything has been a dark void for you for what must have seemed an eternity. But now if our calculations are correct...

(MARLENE holds up the pad. It reads 2+2=X.)

SPIN: ...you can hear and understand me.   Sometimes I think you're the only person on this godforsaken mudball who does understand me. You know Roger, you really are very attractive. I feel like a schoolboy when I'm with you. It may sound foolish, but I think I'm falling in— Oh Roger. Roger, Roger.
You will not believe the day I've had. First my suppliers in Cleveland send me the wrong size biotronic transistors, then I find out the Tesla Institute has cut off all funding for my re-animation project. I swear I am dealing with idiots! Oh, I forgot. Allow me to introduce my associate, Doctor Karl Walker.

MARLENE: *(Into SPIN's mike)* How do you do, Roger Harvey.

SPIN: Anyway, enough about my troubles. I wish there was something I could do right now to ease your pain. Perhaps a song.

(SPIN *serenades* Roger Harvey *while* MARLENE *mixes a*
Dream Express cocktail in a pint glass—Jolt [or Red Bull]
mixed with Nyquil, drinks it down in one gulp, then draws
on her pad, sketching Roger's body-to-be.)

(Music. This song for holiday purposes only.)

SPIN: *(Sings)*
Tinsel makes me tipsy, holly gets me high
I get sloshed on sleigh bells, wrecked when reindeer fly
It's December 25th, the liquor store is closed
But that's okay 'cause I get drunk on Christmas
I get faced on figgy pudding, mauled on mistletoe
Thoughts of old Kris Kringle leave me passed out in
the snow
I don't need no whiskey, rum or bourbon come Noel
I don't need wine 'cause I get drunk on Christmas
Strings of blinking twinkle lights tend to make me tight
I get plastered, plowed, polluted when they play *Silent*
Night
I don't need eggnog, won't go near it, I fill up on
Christmas spirit
I feel just fine when I get drunk on Christmas blah,
blah, blah, blah, blah, blah drunk on Christmas

(End music)

SPIN: Stay strong, my friend. In a few months when
I've perfected the proper equipment, I hope to make it
possible for you to see. And eventually I will present
you with a new electro-mechanical body.

(MARLENE *holds up the pad with a drawing of Roger's brain*
in the jar atop a sexy girl robot body.)

SPIN: And then the two of us can— So have patience,
Roger Harvey. Don't give up hope, and Merry
Christmas. *(He puts away the brain.)*

18.

SPIN: *(Waking Scrooge)* I'm not the man I was. I'm not the man I was…I'm not the man I was…

(Knocking at the door. SPIN opens door. Christmas bells ringing from the street…)

MARLENE: *(As Mrs Dilber)* Good morning, sir.

SPIN: Tell me, what day is it?

MARLENE: What day? Why its Christmas day, o' course.

SPIN: Christmas day! Then I haven't missed it. The curtains are still here. You didn't tear them down and sell them.
I must stand on my head! I must stand on my head!

(Mrs Dilber screams, throws her apron over her own head, keeps screaming.)

SPIN: Please, please Mrs Dilber. I'm not mad—even though I look it.

MARLENE: Don't be violent, sir, or you'll force me to scream for Constable Willie.

SPIN: A fig for Constable Willie. *(Hands her a coin)* Here's a guinea.

MARLENE: A guinea! Here, what for?

SPIN: It's for a Christmas present.

MARLENE: A Christmas present? For me?

SPIN: Of course for you. Dear Mrs Dilber.

MARLENE & SPIN: *(Sing)*
I don't know anything,
I never did know anything,
But now I know that I don't know, All on a Christmas morning.

SPIN: Now you go off and enjoy yourself like a good girl.

MARLENE: Bob's your uncle!

(Christmas bells are still ringing louder and louder.)

MARLENE: Merry Christmas, Mister Scrooge!

(Christmas bells loud, louder and out)

MARLENE: God bless us, every one!

MARLENE & SPIN: Thank you! Thank you! Goodnight! Merry Christmas! Happy Hanukah! Joy in the New year!

19.

It's All Right Now

(Alternative encore)

SPIN: Here's a little dish of figgy pudding to take home with you.

(Music)

MARLENE & SPIN: There she stood, rag and bone
In the Steak and Brew loading zone
Out of luck, busted flat
She's been living in that cowboy hat

He says Hey, I'm your man
We can sleep behind the Fantasy Tan
Two big Macs, got some wine
Moon is high and the night is fine

And its all right now, baby, its all right now
All right now baby, its all right now
(Let me tell you now)

Years go by, sun and rain
Round the curve another passenger train

Sky is red, edge of town
He says honey here's what's going down

Pain inside, I'm all done
Don't want the doctor or the doctor's son
On your way, darling, let me be
Leave me under this sycamore tree

And its all right now, baby, its all right now
All right now baby, its all right now

(Following lines of dialogue are spaced out over the music…)

MARLENE: Sad love story, man.

SPIN: How it goes, baby.

MARLENE: You workin'?

SPIN: Nice jeans. Members Only?

MARLENE: I said, you workin'?

SPIN: Data storage is my line. You a student over the college?

MARLENE: Psych 101, French Lit, *Il pleut dans mon coeur…*

SPIN: These kicks are genuine Florsheim Del-Rays for the casual male.

MARLENE: You want a couple percocet? More where these came from…

SPIN: Dig the buckle.

MARLENE & SPIN: And it's all right now, baby, its all right now yeah. *(Etc)*

(Music ends.)

20.

MARLENE: To help us out on this number, we persuaded the warden out at the Suffolk County Junior Correctional Facility to assign us a couple girls on work-release. Come on up here ladies.

(BACKUP GIRLS *come up, snapping gum etc.*)

ONE GIRL: What you looking at?

www.ingramcontent.com/pod-product-compliance
Lightning Source LLC
Chambersburg PA
CBHW070024110426
42741CB00034B/2445